Blue Mountain Arts®
Bestselling Books

By Susan Polis Schutz:

To My Daughter, with Love, on the Important Things in Life

To My Son, with Love

I Love You

100 Things to Always Remember... and One Thing to Never Forget
by Alin Austin

Is It Time to Make a Change?
by Deanna Beisser

Trust in Yourself
by Donna Fargo

To the One Person I Consider to Be My Soul Mate
by D. Pagels

For You, Just Because You're Very Special to Me
by Collin McCarty

Chasing Away the Clouds
by Douglas Pagels

Anthologies:

42 Gifts I'd Like to Give to You

Always Believe in Yourself and Your Dreams

Creeds of Life, Love, & Inspiration

Follow Your Dreams Wherever They Lead You

For You, My Daughter

Friends Are Forever

Friends for Life

I Love You, Mom

I'm Glad You Are My Sister

The Joys and Challenges of Motherhood

The Language of Recovery ...and Living Life One Day at a Time

Life Can Be Hard Sometimes ...but It's Going to Be Okay

Marriage Is a Promise of Love

May You Always Have an Angel by Your Side

Mottos to Live By

Take Each Day One Step at a Time

There Is Greatness Within You, My Son

These Are the Gifts I'd Like to Give to You

Think Positive Thoughts Every Day

Thoughts of Friendship

Thoughts to Share with a Wonderful Teenager

To My Child

True Friends Always Remain in Each Other's Heart

With God by Your Side ...You Never Have to Be Alone

Words of Love

You're Just like a Sister to Me

TEACHING

and
Learning
Are Lifelong
Journeys

*Thoughts on the Art of Teaching
and the Meaning of Education*

A Blue Mountain Arts® Collection

Blue Mountain Press™

SPS Studios, Inc., Boulder, Colorado

The publisher wishes to acknowledge and thank Tania Lombrozo for her extensive help in compiling the poems and quotations in this collection.

Library of Congress Catalog Card Number: 99-35834
ISBN: 0-88396-522-4

ACKNOWLEDGMENTS appear on page 64.

Certain trademarks are used under license.

Manufactured in China
Third Printing in Hardcover: January 2002

 This book is printed on recycled paper.

Library of Congress Cataloging-in-Publication Data

Teaching & learning are lifelong journeys : thoughts on the art of
    teaching and the meaning of education / a Blue
Mountain Arts collection.
        p.   cm.
    ISBN 0-88396-522-4 (alk. paper)
    1. Education Quotations, maxims, etc.   2. Teaching Quotations,
maxims, etc.   I. SPS Studios (Firm)   II. Title: Teaching
and learning are lifelong journeys.
PN6084.E38T43   1999
370 – dc21   99-35834
                                                     CIP

SPS Studios, Inc.
P.O. Box 4549, Boulder, Colorado 80306

Contents

What Is a Teacher?

A teacher is someone
  who sees each child
as a unique person
and encourages individual
  talents and strengths.

A teacher looks beyond
  each child's face
and sees inside their souls.

A teacher is someone
  with a special touch
and a ready smile
who takes the time
to listen to both sides
and always tries to be fair.

A teacher has a caring heart
that respects and understands.

A teacher is someone
who can look past disruption
  and rebellion,
and recognize hurt and pain.

A teacher teaches the entire child
and helps to build confidence
  and raise self-esteem.

A teacher makes a difference
  in each child's life
and affects each family
and the future of us all.

— Barbara Cage

It is noble to teach oneself; it is still nobler to teach others.

— Mark Twain

To live a single day and hear a good teaching is better than to live a hundred years without knowing such teaching.

— Buddha

I touch the future, I teach.

— Christa McAuliffe

It is the supreme art of the teacher
to awaken joy in creative expression
and knowledge.

— Albert Einstein

Not only is there an art in knowing a
thing, but also a certain art in teaching it.

— Marcus Tullius Cicero

The one exclusive sign of a thorough
knowledge is the power of teaching.

— Aristotle

One looks back with appreciation to the brilliant teachers, but with gratitude to those who touched our human feelings. The curriculum is so much necessary raw material, but warmth is the vital element for the growing plant and for the soul of the child.

– Carl Gustav Jung

A teacher affects eternity; he can never tell where his influence stops.

– Henry Brooks Adams

Knowledge is power.

– Francis Bacon

A teacher should know more than he teaches, and if he knows more than he teaches, he will teach more than he knows.

– Anonymous

What the teacher is, is more important than what he teaches.

– Karl Menninger

The doors of wisdom are never shut.

– Benjamin Franklin

In seeking knowledge, the first step is silence, the second listening, the third remembering, the fourth practicing, and the fifth – teaching others.

– Solomon Ibn Gabirol

Teaching is one of the most crucial, responsible and important professions – since it consists of communicating knowledge and guiding the intellectual development of men. The objective purpose of teaching is the spread and communication of the right ideas, of intellectual values, which means: the creation of a culture.

– Ayn Rand

To know how to suggest is the great art of teaching.

– Henri Frédéric Amiel

How to tell students what to look for without telling them what to see is the dilemma of teaching.

– Lascelles Abercrombie

The important thing is not so much that every child should be taught, as that every child should be given the wish to learn.

– John Lubbock

No man can reveal to you aught but that which already lies half asleep in the dawning of your knowledge.

The teacher who walks in the shadow of the temple, among his followers, gives not of his wisdom but rather of his faith and his lovingness.

If he is indeed wise he does not bid you enter the house of his wisdom, but rather leads you to the threshold of your own mind.

— Kahlil Gibran

The good teacher, the proper teacher, must be ever-living in faith and ever-renewed in creative energy to keep the sap packed in herself, himself, as well as the work.

— Sylvia Plath

It is easy to consider the essential role of creativity in bringing joy and meaning to the human condition – without creativity we have no art, no literature, no science, no innovation, no problem solving, no progress. It is, perhaps, less obvious that creativity has an equally essential role in schools. The processes of creativity parallel those of learning. Recent calls for authentic activities, teaching for understanding, and real world problem solving all require engaging students with content in flexible and innovative ways.

– Alane Jordan Starko

I think we should give children more choices and more power as to what they want to learn, because I do think they want to learn; it is just natural for them, kind of an innate thing, and we need to foster it.

– Kathryn Mongon

If we have a growing human being before us, a child, it is not enough to have certain rules of how he should be taught and educated, and then just conform to the rules as one does in a technical science. This will never lead to good teaching. We must bring an inner fire, an inner enthusiasm, to our work; we must have impulses which are not intellectually transmitted from teacher to child according to certain rules, but which pass over from teacher to child in an intimate way. The whole of our being must work in us as educators, not only the thinking man; the man of feeling and the man of will must also play their part.

— Rudolf Steiner

It is a general insight, which merits more attention than it receives, that teaching should not be compared to filling a bottle with water but rather to helping a flower to grow in its own way. As any good teacher knows, the methods of instruction and the range of material covered are matters of small importance as compared with the success in arousing the natural curiosity of the students and stimulating their interest in exploring on their own.

— Noam Chomsky

Learning is by nature curiosity.

— Philo

There is no teaching until the pupil is brought into the same state or principle in which you are; a transfusion takes place; he is you and you are he; then is a teaching, and by no unfriendly chance or bad company can he ever quite lose the benefit.

– Ralph Waldo Emerson

It is that openness and awareness and innocence of sorts that I try to cultivate in my dancers. Although, as the Latin verb to educate, *educere,* indicates, it is not a question of putting something in but drawing it out, if it is there to begin with.... I want all of my students and all of my dancers to be aware of the poignancy of life at that moment. I would like to feel that I had, in some way, given them the gift of themselves.

– Martha Graham

Knowledge cannot be poured into the child's mind, like fluid from one vessel into another. The pupil may do something by intuition, but generally there must be a conscious effort on his part. He is not a passive recipient, but an active, voluntary agent. He must do more than admit or welcome; he must reach out, and grasp, and bring home. It is the duty of the teacher to bring knowledge within arm's length of the learner; and he must break down its masses into portions so minute, that they can be taken up and appropriated, one by one; but the final appropriating act must be the learner's.

A desire of learning is better than all external opportunities, because it will find or make opportunities, and then improve them.

– Horace Mann

To Teach Is to Hope

To teach is to hope...
that one day a child will know
the meaning of confidence
and be able to touch other lives.

To teach is to pray...
that these newly brave souls will
   use their talents
to better the world,
instead of just themselves.

To teach is to feel...
that not all the hurts
   of those in our care
      can be healed,
but they can be soothed.

— Mary Swiatkowski

I have always had a fancy that learning might be
made a play and recreation to children; and that
they might be brought to desire to be taught, if it
were proposed to them as a thing of honor, credit,
delight, and recreation, or as a reward for doing
something else, and if they were never corrected
for the neglect of it.

— John Locke

A classroom for a young child is a life
world; each year brings new forms of
power, of possibility.... As educators
we are responsible for making school a
place in which a child matters — a place
away from the edges.

— V. Polokow

I think that part of what you need to do to be a good teacher is to be able to imagine the lives of your students and to respond compassionately to that and through that compassionate response make a decision that they are worthwhile and that they are bringing something to the experience and that you as the teacher have an important role in shaping them.

– David Haynes

The teacher will, in his profession, be able to draw his own inspiration out of the feeling of his relationship to the world and to his own being, just like the artist who has the work of art in his very marrow.

– Rudolf Steiner

The successful teacher is no longer on a height, pumping knowledge at high pressure into passive receptacles…. He is a senior student anxious to help his juniors.

– Sir William Osler

Learning without thought is labor lost;
thought without learning is perilous.

— Confucius

A man who is pleased when he receives
good instruction will sleep peacefully, because
his mind is thereby cleansed.

— Buddha

It is better to know nothing than
to learn nothing.

— Hebrew Proverb

In teaching children we must seek
insensibly to unite knowledge with
the carrying out of that knowledge
into practice.

– Immanuel Kant

In seed time learn, in harvest teach,
in winter enjoy.

– William Blake

And gladly would ye lerne,
and gladly teche.

– Geoffrey Chaucer

In searching for the fundamental principles of the science of teaching, I find few axioms as indisputable as are the first principles of mathematics. One of these is this, He Is The Best Teacher Who Makes The Best Use Of His Own Time And That Of His Pupils. For Time is all that is given by God in which to do the work of improvement.

— Emma Hart Willard

There are lazy minds as well as lazy bodies.

— Benjamin Franklin

Every day is lost
in which
we do not
learn something useful.
Man has no nobler
or more valuable
possession than time.

— Ludwig van Beethoven

If a man keeps cherishing his old knowledge, so as continually to be acquiring new, he may be a teacher of others.

— Confucius

If you have knowledge, let others light their candles at it.

— Margaret Fuller

Imparting knowledge is only lighting other men's candles at our lamp without depriving ourselves of any flame.

— Jane Porter

I think that by far the most important bill in our whole code is that for the diffusion of knowledge among the people. No other sure foundation can be devised for the preservation of freedom, and happiness.

— Thomas Jefferson

Schools… are the most effective means of developing and training those powers and faculties in a child, by which, when he becomes a man, he may understand what his highest interests and his highest duties are; and may be, in fact, and not in name only, a free agent.

— Horace Mann

The objects of primary education:

To give every citizen the information he needs for the transaction of his own business;

To enable him to calculate for himself, and to express and preserve his ideas, his contracts and accounts, in writing;

To improve, by reading, his morals and faculties;

To understand his duties to his neighbors and country, and to discharge with competence the functions confided to him by either;

To know his rights; to exercise with order and justice those he retains; to choose with discretion the fiduciary of those he delegates; and to notice their conduct with diligence, with candor, and judgment;

And, in general, to observe with intelligence and faithfulness all the social relations under which he shall be placed.

– Thomas Jefferson .

The teacher is engaged, not simply in the training of the individual, but in the formation of the proper social life.

I believe that every teacher should realize the dignity of his calling, that he is a social servant set apart for the maintenance of proper social order and the securing of the right social growth.

I believe that in this way the teacher always is the prophet of the true God and the usherer in of the true kingdom of God.

— John Dewey

What people need and what they want may be very different.... Teachers are those who educate the people to appreciate the things they need.

— Elbert Hubbard

The future of the nation is on the shoulders of teachers and how they teach kids; the future of the world is in the classroom where the teachers are. And if we have any chance to guarantee a positive bridge to the 21st century, it is how we educate the children in the classrooms today.

– Richard Reginald Green

It is through good education that all the good in the world arises.

– Immanuel Kant

Plants are fashioned by cultivation,
men by education. We are born feeble
and need strength; possessing nothing,
we need assistance; beginning without
intelligence, we need judgment. All
that we lack at birth and need when
grown up is given us by education.

– Jean Jacques Rousseau

A child without education is poorer and more
wretched than a man without bread.

– Horace Mann

Genius without Education
is like Silver in the Mine.

– Benjamin Franklin

Teachers are secondary only to parents in kids' lives, and sometimes they are the primary adult because of the huge amount of time children spend in school.

— Kathryn Mongon

A teacher is one of the most special people in the world, for who else could spend day after day giving of themselves to someone else's children?

— Deanna Beisser

Teaching seems to me beyond doubt the greatest of the professions.

— Theodore Brameld

The best teacher will be he who has at his
tongue's end the explanation of what it is that
is bothering the pupil. These explanations give
the teacher the knowledge of the greatest possible
number of methods, the ability of inventing new
methods, and, above all, not a blind adherence to
one method, but the conviction that all methods
are one-sided, and that the best method would
be the one which would answer best to all the
possible difficulties incurred by a pupil, that is,
not a method, but an art and talent.

— Leo Tolstoy

Education has for its object
the formation of character.

— Herbert Spencer

The best method for a given teacher is the one which is most familiar to the teacher.

— Leo Tolstoy

There is no such whetstone, to sharpen a good wit and encourage a will to learning, as is praise.

— Roger Ascham

Teaching should be such that what is offered is perceived as a valuable gift and not as a hard duty.

— Albert Einstein

As a Teacher...

... I think it's so important to understand and get to know children for who they are and what's important to them and know what their life is like. It's so important to have time where you can connect one on one with each child, where you take fifteen minutes and sit down and talk with this student about what life is like this week and what they're thinking about and just really get to know them.

— Kathryn Mongon

... I want to know more about the worlds my students bring into the classroom with them.... [If] teaching is to be a creative process... I have to listen.

— Carol Stumbo

... Only one resource is at my immediate command: my identity, my selfhood, my sense of this "I" who teaches – without which I have no sense of the "Thou" who learns.

— Parker J. Palmer

... I try to be really aware [of differences among students], and I am always working on it. I am not very critical of other people... you have to be nonjudgmental. You have to be supportive. To me that is how you deliver messages and change minds.

— Bill Simpson

My stance as a teacher is tied to all I am as a human being. Who I am and how I am permeate the classroom. No matter what subject we teach, we teach and live what we value. What we value is woven throughout the textures of who we are as human beings, and who we are as teachers. We are the curriculum. Our students are the curriculum. None of our students remember the enumerable times we reminded them, and continue to remind them, that *a lot* is not one word; or wrote out for the umpteenth time the difference between *their, they're,* and *there*; or how they felt as they read some inane passage on the standardized test and filled in the blanks with a date or a part of speech. What they do remember are the times we were honest with each other as human beings, because in those moments of showing honest emotion we formed relationships.

— Linda Rief

As a Parent...

I leave my child with you
each day that you may instill in him all
the concepts of life.
You teach him sharing
so he understands nothing is of
value unless it is shared.
You teach him art so the radiant
colors of the world will not pass him by.
You teach him letters so words
may become his tool to help make
this planet a gentler place.
You teach him time so he comes
to know nothing lasts forever,
especially childhood...
You teach him about acceptance
so he learns not all of life is fair.
You are my child's teacher, and
there is no better thing to be.

– Robyn Keough

Good Teachers Make
Being a Parent
a Little Easier

Being a parent isn't always easy.
It's such a big responsibility
to direct another person's life —
you often wonder
if you're doing everything right.
I imagine that teachers
feel some of the same things
that parents do.
Though their work is to teach,
they do more than that.
They are counselors, role models,
and often friends.
They are to be thanked
for all they do
to make a parent's job
a little easier.

— Taylor MacKenzie

As a Student...

... It isn't always easy,
and there are times when you
could give up, but you don't.
You continue working hard,
making sacrifices of time and fun,
and wondering if it will ever be worth it.
And it is because
you learn some important
    lessons in life –
like how to get along with others,
that trying is often as important
    as succeeding,
that mistakes are okay as long as
    you learn from them,
that you can accomplish your goals,
and that you can make your future
    anything you want it to be.

– Barbara Cage

... It takes a lot to set your sights on a distant horizon
and keep on reaching for your goals. It takes a lot... of
courage and hard work, believing and achieving, patience
and perseverance, inner strength and gentle hope. It takes a
lot of giving it your best, and it takes continuing to learn as
long as you live.

– Alin Austin

Knowledge is not what you learn,
but what you remember....
It is not what you study, but what you
remember and reflect upon, that makes
you learned.

— Schuyler Colfax

In studying Law or Physics, or any other
Art or Science, by which you propose to get
your Livelihood, though you find it at first hard,
difficult and unpleasing, use Diligence, Patience
and Perseverance; the Irksomeness of your
Task will thus diminish daily, and your Labor
shall finally be crowned with Success.

— Benjamin Franklin

What matters is not
how many high grades you've
earned, but if you've been
inspired by what you've learned.

— Jacqueline Schiff

A Good Teacher Encourages You to Want to Learn

A good teacher is someone who
directs and instructs,
but never demands that a student learn.
A good teacher challenges your mind
and provides you with opportunities
to gain knowledge at your own speed.
A good teacher encourages you to ask questions,
even if your ideas are not completely correct.
A good teacher teaches from the heart
with an inner sense of desire for others
to also enjoy the mysteries of the universe.
For a good teacher is not necessarily
a leader to be followed,
but a guide who suggests and leaves you
to carry on down your own road.

— Laura Medley

Where there is much desire to learn,
there of necessity will be
much arguing, much writing, many
opinions; for opinion in good men
is but knowledge in the making.

— John Milton

Must we always teach our children
with books?

Let them look at the mountains and the stars
up above. Let them look at the beauty of
the waters and the trees and flowers on earth.

They will then begin to think, and
to think is the beginning of a real education.

— David Polis

I went to the woods because
I wished to live deliberately,
to front only the essential
facts of life, and see if I
could not learn what it had to teach,
and not, when I came to die,
discover that I had not lived.

— Henry David Thoreau

A love of learning doesn't stop with graduation.
Your whole life will be a learning and growing
experience, whose extent can only be imagined.
Life will be your classroom.

— Donna Gephart

Much have I learned from my teachers, more from my colleagues, but most from my students.

– Talmud: Ta'anith, 7b

The bad teacher's words fall on his pupils like harsh rain; the good teacher's, as gently as the dew.

– Talmud: Ta'anith, 7a

Education makes a man a more intelligent shoemaker, if that be his occupation, but not by teaching him how to make shoes; it does so by the mental exercise it gives, and the habits it impresses.

– John Stuart Mill

The true teacher defends his pupils against his own personal influence. He inspires self-trust. He guides their eyes from himself to the spirit that quickens him. He will have no disciple.

– Amos Bronson Alcott

Any piece of knowledge which the pupil has himself acquired – any problem which he has himself solved, becomes, by virtue of the conquest, much more thoroughly his than it could else be. The preliminary activity of mind which his success implies, the concentration of thought necessary to it, and the excitement consequent on his triumph, conspire to register the facts in his memory in a way that no mere information heard from a teacher, or read in a schoolbook, can be registered.

– Herbert Spencer

Education is not the filling of a pail, but the lighting of a fire.

– William Butler Yeats

All of our teachers: how bright in our mind,
We recall every one, as they came;
Each, like a wise monarch, unselfish and kind,
Did make our advancement their aim.
Think not that the scholar, ne'er valued thy care;
Thy teachings sank deeper than thou wert aware.

— Priscilla Jane Thompson

For rigorous teachers seized my youth,
And purged its faith, and trimmed its fire,
Showed me the high, white star of Truth,
There bade me gaze, and there aspire.

— Matthew Arnold

To teachers, students are the end products, – all else is a means. Hence there is but one interpretation of high standards in teaching: standards are highest where the maximum number of students – slow learners and fast learners alike – develop to their maximal capacity.

– Joseph Seidlin

I can easier teach twenty what were good to be done, than be one of the twenty to follow mine own teaching.

– William Shakespeare

The man who can make hard things easy is the educator.

— Ralph Waldo Emerson

Part of teaching is helping students learn how to tolerate ambiguity, consider possibilities, and ask questions that are unanswerable.

— Sara Lawrence Lightfoot

Education is the ability to listen to almost anything without losing your temper or your self-confidence.

— Robert Frost

As teachers, we invest a great deal of our professional, intellectual lives trying to see beneath the surface of what we encounter. What drives our curiosity is trying to understand core phenomena or motivations that give rise to what we see. That is, we try, even if we don't always succeed, to be attentive and insightful learners.

– Roald Hoffmann and Brian Coppola

Teachers and learners are correlates, one of which was never intended to be without the other.

– Jonathan Edwards

To be a teacher in the right sense is to be a learner. Instruction begins when you, the teacher, learn from the learner, put yourself in his place so that you may understand what he understands and in the way he understands it.

— Søren Kierkegaard

It is a luxury to learn; but the luxury of learning is not to be compared with the luxury of teaching.

— R. D. Hitchcock

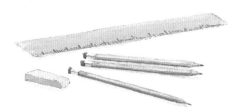

He who constantly aids children to their ends, hourly provides them with the satisfaction of conquest, hourly encourages them through their difficulties and sympathizes in their successes, will be liked; nay, if his behavior is consistent throughout, must be loved.

– Herbert Spencer

We should not be speaking to, but with. That is second nature to any good teacher.

– Noam Chomsky

Any teacher can study books, but books do not necessarily bring wisdom, nor that human insight essential to consummate teaching skills.

— Bliss Perry

We don't know one millionth of one percent about anything.

— Thomas A. Edison

Teachers learn from their students' discussions.

— Rashi

The aim of education should not be to teach how to use human energies to improve the environment, for we are finally beginning to realize that the cornerstone of education is the development of the human personality, and that in this regard education is of immediate importance for the salvation of mankind.

— Maria Montessori

In teaching, we do not impose our wills on the student, but introduce him to the many mansions of the heritage in which we ourselves strive to live, and to the improvement of which we are ourselves dedicated.

— Israel Scheffler

Only the brave should teach. Only those who love the young should teach. Teaching is a vocation. It is as sacred as priesthood; as innate a desire, as inescapable as the genius which compels a great artist. If he has not the concern for humanity, the love of living creatures, the vision of the priest and the artist, he must not teach.

— Pearl S. Buck

The essence of education is not to stuff you with facts but to help you discover your uniqueness, to teach you how to develop it, and then to show you how to give it away.

— Leo Buscaglia

Teaching Is
a Lifelong Journey

To teach is to touch the lives of many
and to help us learn life's lessons.
But to teach <u>well</u> is to make a difference
in all the lives you touch.

To teach is to be a parent, nurse, friend,
    and confidant;
to be a supporter, a leader, and a motivator.
But to teach <u>well</u>
    is to be all of these things,
yet not lose sight of who you are.
You share a part of yourself
with all whose lives
you have touched.

To teach is to be tender,
loving, strong, and giving
to all who rely upon you;
to encourage and praise.
But to teach <u>well</u>
is to believe in what
and whom you teach.

A teacher comes to master
  these many jobs
throughout the years.
But those who teach <u>well</u>
recognize that there
will always be more
to learn in life's journey,
and they never hesitate
to strive to learn it.

— Donna Bulger

A teacher who can arouse a feeling for one single good action, for one single good poem, accomplishes more than he who fills our memory with rows and rows of natural objects, classified with name and form.

– Johann Wolfgang von Goethe

Good teaching is one-fourth preparation and three-fourths theatre.

– Gail Godwin

You go into an audience and ask people to go back over their childhood and pick out the teachers that did the most for them. I think you will find in every case that they will say such and such a teacher waked them up, or such and such a teacher first inspired them. They will put it in different ways. They may have forgotten whether she was a good disciplinarian or not. The mechanical teachers will not be the ones they will speak of; it will be the teachers that roused them, that got hold of them. That means the teacher that found out the mental trait that was uppermost in the pupil, and that succeeded in giving it intellectual nutriment in such a way as to make it grow. The child did not know this trait. The other teachers did not find it out; but through some natural instinct, this particular teacher divined what was going on in that mind and succeeded in making connections.

That is the great object of education.

– John Dewey

Education should never work against a person's destiny, but should achieve the full development of his own predispositions. The education of a man today so often lags behind the talents and tendencies which his destiny has implanted in him. We must keep pace with these powers to such an extent that the human being in our care can win his way through to all that his destiny will allow – to the fullest clarity of thought, the most loving deepening of his feeling, and the greatest possible energy and ability of will.

This can only be done by an art of education and teaching which is based on a real knowledge of man.

– Rudolf Steiner

Both teaching and rational inquiry,
at their creative and inspired best,
thus lead us to the very threshold of
ultimate mystery and induce in us a
sense of profound humility and awe.

– Theodore Meyer Greene

As teachers we must believe in change, must know it is possible, or we wouldn't be teaching — because education is a constant process of change. Every single time you "teach" something to someone, it is ingested, something is done with it, and a new human being emerges.

— Leo Buscaglia

Teachers are like flowers:
they spread their beauty
throughout the world.
Their love of learning
touches the hearts of their students,
who then carry that sense of wonder
with them wherever they may go.
Teachers, with their words of wisdom,
awaken the spirit within us all
and lead us down the roads of life.

— Deanna Beisser

A Message of Thanks to All the Great Teachers in This World

Thank you for being such wonderful teachers, exemplary role models, and caring people. Thank you for knowing your subjects and sharing your knowledge. Thank you for not being afraid to treat students like real people. Thank you for showing acceptance, approval, and appreciation. These are all gifts that are so important to a student's development and that your students will always remember, just as they will also remember you.

Words of encouragement, a little respect, and simple gestures of kindness from a teacher promote the perfect climate for students to study, learn, and grow. Your attitude translates into a spirit of friendliness and good will toward others in a sometimes unfriendly world. Progress is easier in an atmosphere of creative freedom, joy, and ease, and you foster this feeling in your classroom.

I salute the good work you've done. I appreciate the people you are, and I thank you for your positive influence. You have passed on invaluable instruction and wisdom and created pleasurable moments associated with learning that will always be sweet memories.

Thank you for answering the call to be teachers. Thank you for the enduring impression you've made in the lives you have touched. Every community needs people like you. Your contributions are immeasurable. Your lessons are permanent. You improve our world. You are so important.

— Donna Fargo

Teaching is a process of becoming that continues throughout life, never completely achieved, never completely denied. This is the challenge and the fun of being a teacher — there is no ultimate end to the process.

— Frances Mayforth

Education is not a preparation for life; education is life itself.

— John Dewey

The teachers of this country, one may say, have its future in their hands.

— William James

God Bless the Teacher

God bless the teacher...
For in your care each day,
you teach the children
to laugh and play and enjoy
their lives that are
still unspoiled by a world
that is sometimes hard to understand.

God bless the teacher...
You build your students'
hopes and dreams and self-esteem.
You teach them compassion, friendship, and loyalty.
You help them grow and teach them things
that matter most.
You teach them how to be themselves.

God bless the teacher...
For being there
to calm your students' fears,
cheer them up, and dry their tears.
Thank you for everything you do.

— Julia Escobar

ACKNOWLEDGMENTS

We gratefully acknowledge the permission granted by the following authors, publishers, and authors' representatives to reprint poems or excerpts from their publications.

Random House, Inc. for "I touch the..." by Christa McAuliffe from I TOUCH THE FUTURE: THE STORY OF CHRISTA MCAULIFFE by Robert T. Hohler. Copyright © 1987 by Random House, Inc. All rights reserved.

Wayne State University Press for "It is the supreme..." by Albert Einstein, "How to tell..." by Lascelles Abercrombie, and "To be a..." by Søren Kierkegaard, and "Only the brave..." by Pearl S. Buck from QUOTABLE QUOTES ON EDUCATION by August Kerber. Copyright © 1968 by Wayne State University Press.

Gale Research for "One looks back..." by Carl Gustav Jung, and "Part of teaching..." by Sara Lawrence Lightfoot. Taken from GALE'S QUOTATIONS edited by Shelly Dickie. Copyright © 1995 by Gale Research, Inc. All rights reserved.

Dutton, a division of Penguin Putnam, Inc., for "Teaching is one..." from LETTERS OF AYN RAND edited by Michael Berliner. Copyright © 1995 by The Estate of Ayn Rand. Introduction Copyright © 1995 by Leonard Peikoff.

Alfred A. Knopf, Inc. and Gibran National Committee for "No man can..." from THE PROPHET by Kahlil Gibran. Copyright © 1923 by Kahlil Gibran, renewal copyright © 1951 by Administrators C.T.A. of Kahlil Gibran Estate, and Mary G. Gibran. All rights reserved.

Doubleday, a division of Bantam Doubleday Dell Publishing Group, Inc., and Faber & Faber, Ltd. for "The good teacher..." from THE JOURNALS OF SYLVIA PLATH edited by Ted Hughes. Copyright © 1982 by Ted Hughes as Executor of The Estate of Sylvia Plath. For "It is that openness..." from BLOOD MEMORY by Martha Graham. Copyright © 1991 by Martha Graham Estate. All rights reserved.

Allyn and Bacon for "It is easy to..." from CREATIVITY IN THE CLASSROOM by Alane Jordan Starko. Copyright © 1995 by Longman Publishers USA. All rights reserved.

State University of New York Press for "I think we should...," "Teachers are secondary...," and "I think it's so..." by Kathryn Mongon; "I think that part..." by David Haynes; and "I try to be really..." by Bill Simpson from TEACHERS' READING/TEACHERS' LIVES by Mary Kay Rummel and Elizabeth P. Quintero. Copyright © 1997 by State University of New York. All rights reserved.

The MIT Press for "It is a general..." from LANGUAGE AND PROBLEMS OF KNOWLEDGE: THE MAGNA LECTURES by Noam Chomsky. Copyright © 1988 Massachusetts Institute of Technology. All rights reserved.

University of Chicago Press for "A classroom for a..." from LIVES ON THE EDGE: SINGLE MOTHERS AND THEIR CHILDREN IN THE OTHER AMERICA by V. Polokow. Copyright © 1993 by University of Chicago Press. All rights reserved.

The University of Michigan Press for "In teaching children..." from EDUCATION by Immanuel Kant, published by Ann Arbor Paperbacks. Copyright © 1960 by Ann Arbor Paperbacks. All rights reserved.

Johnson Publishing for "The future of..." by Richard Reginald Green from EBONY MAGAZINE. Copyright © 1988 by Ebony Magazine. All rights reserved.

Teachers College Press for "Education has for...," "Any piece of...," and "He who constantly..." by Herbert Spencer from HERBERT SPENCER ON EDUCATION edited by A. M. Kazamias. Copyright © 1966 by Teachers College, Columbia University. All rights reserved. pp.179,181.

The New York Times for "Teaching should be..." by Albert Einstein from THE NEW YORK TIMES, October 5, 1952. Copyright © 1952 by the New York Times Co. All rights reserved.

Harvard Educational Review for "I want to know..." from "Beyond the Classroom" by Carol Stumbo, HARVARD EDUCATIONAL REVIEW, 59:1 (Spring1989), pp.87-97. Copyright © 1989 by the President and Fellows of Harvard College. All rights reserved.

Jossey-Bass, Inc., Publishers for "Only one resource..." from THE COURAGE TO TEACH by Parker J. Palmer. Copyright © 1998 by Jossey-Bass, Inc., Publishers. All rights reserved.

Heinemann, a division of Reed Elsevier, Inc., for "My stance as a teacher..." by Linda Rief from ALL THAT MATTERS edited by Linda Rief and Maureen Barbieri. Copyright © 1995 by Heinemann. All rights reserved.

Southern Illinois University Press for "What the teacher..." by Karl Menninger; "To teachers, students..." by Joseph Seidlin; "Any teacher can study..." by Bliss Perry; and "Teaching seems to..." by Theodore Brameld from AND MERELY TEACH by Arthur E. Lean. Copyright © 1968 by Southern Illinois University Press. All rights reserved.

National Science Teachers Association Publications for "As teachers..." by Roald Hoffmann and Brian Coppola from THE JOURNAL OF COLLEGE SCIENCE TEACHING. Copyright © 1996 by National Science Teachers Association, 1840 Wilson Boulevard, Arlington, VA 22201-3000. All rights reserved.

South End Press for "We should not..." from POWERS AND PROSPECTS: REFLECTIONS ON HUMAN NATURE AND THE SOCIAL ORDER by Noam Chomsky. Copyright © 1996 by South End Press. All rights reserved.

Regnery Publishing, Inc. for "The aim of..." from EDUCATION AND PEACE by Maria Montessori. Copyright © 1972 by Mario M. Montessori. All rights reserved.

Harvard University Press for "In teaching, we..." from "Philosophical Models of Teaching" by Israel Scheffler, HARVARD EDUCATIONAL REVIEW 35:2 (Spring 1965) p. 143. All rights reserved.

The Felice Foundation for "The essence of..." and "As teachers we..." from LIVING, LOVING & LEARNING by Leo Buscaglia, Ph.D., published by Ballantine Books. Copyright © 1982 by Leo F. Buscaglia, Inc. All rights reserved.

Random House, Inc. for "Good teaching is..." from THE GOOD WOMAN by Gail Godwin. Copyright © 1974 by Gail Godwin. All rights reserved.

PrimaDonna Entertainment Corp. for "A Message of Thanks to All the Great Teachers in This World" by Donna Fargo. Copyright © 1999 by PrimaDonna Entertainment Corp. All rights reserved.

Deanna Beisser for "One of the most...." Copyright © 1999 by Deanna Beisser. All rights reserved.

Donna Bulger for "Teaching Is a Lifelong Journey." Copyright © 1999 by Donna Bulger. All rights reserved.

Julia Escobar for "God Bless the Teacher." Copyright © 1999 by Julia Escobar. All rights reserved.

Mary Swiatkowski for "To Teach Is to Touch." Copyright © 1999 by Mary Swiatkowski. All rights reserved.

Robyn Keough for "I leave my child...." Copyright © 1999 by Robyn Keough. All rights reserved.

Jacqueline Schiff for "What matters is not...." Copyright © 1999 by Jacqueline Schiff. All rights reserved.

Donna Gephart for "A love of learning...." Copyright © 1999 by Donna Gephart. All rights reserved.

Laura Medley for "A Good Teacher Encourages You to Want to Learn." Copyright © 1999 by Laura Medley. All rights reserved.

A careful attempt has been made to trace the ownership of selections used in this anthology in order to obtain permission to reprint copyrighted materials and give proper credit to the copyright owners. If any error or omission has occurred, it is completely inadvertent, and we would like to make corrections in future editions provided that written notification is made to the publisher:

SPS STUDIOS, INC., P.O. Box 4549, Boulder, Colorado 80306